Tinker Bell Takes Charge

Tinker Bell Takes Charge

WRITTEN BY
ELEANOR FREMONT

ILLUSTRATED BY
THE DISNEY STORYBOOK ARTISTS

HarperCollins *Children's Books*

First published in the USA by Disney Press,
114 Fifth Avenue, New York, New York, 10011-5690.

First published in Great Britain in 2006
by HarperCollins Children's Books.
HarperCollins Children's Books is a division of
HarperCollins Publishers,
77 - 85 Fulham Palace Road, Hammersmith, London, W6 8JB.

The HarperCollins Children's Books website is
www.harpercollinschildrensbooks.co.uk

978-0-00-721403-7
0-00-721403-0

1 2 3 4 5 6 7 8 9 10

Printed and bound in the UK

Visit disneyfairies.com

This book is proudly printed on paper which contains wood
from well managed forests, certified in accordance with
the rules of the Forest Stewardship Council.
For more information about FSC,
please visit www.fsc-uk.org

Mixed Sources
Product group from well-managed
forests and other controlled sources
www.fsc.org   Cert no. SW-COC-1806
FSC   © 1996 Forest Stewardship Council

All About Fairies

IF YOU HEAD toward the second star on your right and fly straight on till morning, you'll come to Never Land, a magical island where mermaids play and children never grow up.

When you arrive, you might hear something like the tinkling of little bells. Follow that sound and you'll find Pixie Hollow, the secret heart of Never Land.

A great old maple tree grows in Pixie Hollow, and in it live hundreds of fairies and sparrow men. Some of them can do water magic, others can fly like the wind, and still others can speak to animals. You see, Pixie Hollow is the Never fairies' kingdom, and each fairy who lives there has a special, extraordinary talent.

Not far from the Home Tree, nestled in the branches of a hawthorn, is Mother Dove, the most magical creature of all. She sits on her egg, watching over the fairies, who in turn watch over her. For as long as Mother Dove's egg stays well and whole, no one in Never Land will ever grow old.

Once, Mother Dove's egg *was* broken. But we are not telling the story of the egg here. Now it is time for Tinker Bell's tale…

Tinker Bell Takes Charge

1

IT WAS A MILD, sunny day in Pixie Hollow – a perfect sort of a day. Little white clouds scampered across a dazzling blue sky. A soft breeze rustled the leaves of the Home Tree, the great ageless maple where the Never fairies lived.

Although it was a perfect day, Tinker Bell was not in her usual high spirits. Something was bothering her, but she could not figure out what it was. She wasn't sick. She wasn't sad. It was more like she had an itch that she couldn't find, let alone scratch.

Just that morning, she had caught sight of her face in the polished walls of the Home Tree's lobby. She'd noticed her slumped shoulders and the frown on her face. Even her ponytail drooped.

This troublesome feeling was on her mind now as she flew toward her bedroom, which was high in the branches of the Home Tree. She needed to change her shoes before she could go back to her workshop. The ones she was wearing had gotten soaked on a visit to Thistle's strawberry patch. Thistle, a garden-talent fairy, had asked Tink to look at a garden hoe that needed fixing. It had been left on the damp ground among the strawberries, and the blade had rusted through. It would have to be replaced. *But it will be easy to fix*, Tink thought.

She headed up through the trunk of the Home Tree. The trunk split into branches. She turned right, then left, then left again, winding upward. The corridor narrowed as the tree's limbs tapered.

Tink's bedroom was at the end of one of the topmost branches. When the hallway was so tight that her head nearly grazed the ceiling, she reached the door to her room.

As soon as she was inside, her spirits lifted a bit. Tink loved her room. Everything in it reflected her talent and personality. There was her beloved bed, which was made from a pirate's metal loaf pan. There were the lampshades made from old colanders. Even the chair she was sitting on was special. The back of it was made from a serving platter, the seat was a frying pan, and the legs were made from old serving spoons.

At one point or another, Tink had repaired the frying pan, the platter, and each of the spoons. Some she had repaired more than once. But eventually, pans and spoons wore out. Although Tink thought anything broken could be fixed, the kitchen-talent fairies didn't always agree. Sometimes they threw their worn-out pots and platters away.

Tink felt a special connection with every pot and pan she'd ever fixed. She couldn't bear to see any of them on the scrap-metal heap. So when the kitchen-talent fairies had thrown out the pan, the platter, and the spoons, she'd rescued them and brought them back to her workshop. With a lot of thought and a few pinches of fairy dust, she'd turned them into a chair.

Tink thought about the frying-pan chair as she closed the door to her room and flew back down through the Home Tree. What a wonderful challenge it had been to make. Not like fixing Thistle's silly rusted hoe. There was nothing hard about replacing a hoe blade. No challenge at all.

Suddenly Tink stopped in her tracks.

"That's it!" she said aloud. "That is what's bothering me! No challenge!"

Tink was one of the best pots-and-pans-talent fairies in all of Pixie Hollow. Her joy came from fixing things. She liked a challenging problem more than almost anything.

But for weeks now, every job Tink had been given had been as easy as gooseberry pie. No pots that wouldn't boil water. No colanders that refused to drain. No pans that were more hole than pan. Just "fix this little hole, fix that little hole." Boring, boring, boring.

But at least now I know what's wrong, Tink thought. *What I need is a problem to solve! A big one!*

"Tink!" A voice behind her interrupted her thoughts. Tink turned. Her good friend Rani, a water-talent fairy, was hurrying toward her.

Being the only fairy without wings,

Rani could not fly. So Tink gently landed on the moss carpet in the Home Tree's hallway. She waited until Rani caught up.

"Where are you going?" Rani asked.

"I was just on my way back to my workshop," Tink replied. "Why do you – "

"Ask?" said Rani. She had a habit of finishing everyone's sentences. "No big reason. I just thought maybe we could play a game of – "

But Rani never got to finish. At that moment, she was interrupted by a tremendous crash. Both fairies heard branches cracking and snapping near the top of the Home Tree.

In the next instant, there was a *thud* that shook the tree to its very roots. Tink and Rani nearly lost their balance.

From the nearby tearoom came the sound of dishes falling and shattering.

Then there was silence.

Tink and Rani stared at each other.

"Did the moon just fall out of the sky?" Rani whispered in awe.

"Maybe it was a branch falling from another tree," said Tink. But even as she spoke, she knew that wasn't it. The sound had been made by something very heavy and solid. And it had landed quite close by.

"Maybe a great big bird just came in for a landing," said Rani.

"Maybe," said Tink. But that didn't seem right either.

The two fairies listened carefully. After a long moment Tink took a deep breath and straightened her shoulders.

"We've got to go and see – "

"What it is. If you say so," said Rani. She dabbed her forehead with a leafkerchief and attempted to smile bravely. Though they were both nervous, it was a lot easier to see it on Rani. She was the most watery of all the water-talent fairies. At the moment, her forehead was beaded with sweat.

The two fairies headed back toward the front entrance of the Home Tree. Tink walked so that she wouldn't get too far ahead of Rani. Brave as she was, even Tink didn't want to go outside alone. Together they hurried past the tearoom, down the corridor, through the lobby, and out the knothole door.

When Tink stepped into the sunlight, she stopped cold and gasped.

Rani, who was right on Tink's heels, crashed into her.

Rani peeked over Tink's shoulder. She gasped, too.

"*What* is *that?*" she whispered.

2

RIGHT IN FRONT of them was a huge, menacing-looking black ball. It was taller than two fairies put together and just as wide. It had landed right in the middle of the Home Tree's courtyard.

A large crack ran through the courtyard where it had smashed down. Several toadstool chairs had been damaged or squashed completely. The ground around the ball was covered with the splintered remains of branches and twigs.

Tink's mind reeled. The courtyard was a very special place for the fairies. Many of their most important meetings and celebrations were held there. Not to mention, the fairies had to fly through it to reach the Home Tree's knothole door.

Whenever Tink saw the courtyard, she felt that she was home. It always seemed to say, "Welcome. The Home Tree waits to embrace you." Now the sight of the damaged courtyard made her heart ache.

A large crowd of fairies had gathered around the ball. Clarion, the fairy queen, stepped forward.

"Is everyone all right?" she asked. Her voice was tense with worry. "Is anyone hurt?"

Noses and wings were quickly counted, amid a buzz of concern. Incredibly, every fairy in the Home Tree had escaped harm.

The queen sighed with relief. She looked around the crowd. "Terence,

Spring, Jerome, Rosetta, Luna," she said. Her voice had regained its normal regal tone. The fairies and sparrow men sprang to attention. "Fly to the top of the tree and see what damage has been done. Please report back at once."

With Terence, a fairy-dust-talent sparrow man, in the lead, the group took off.

When they had gone, a scullery-talent fairy tiptoed up to the great ball. She raised her hand as if to touch its rough surface. But at the last second she pulled her hand back. "Do you think it might be alive?" she whispered.

All at once, the fairies nearest to the ball hopped back a couple of steps.

"What's it made of?" asked Dulcie, a baking-talent fairy.

The fairies around her shook their heads, muttering, "Don't know."

"Maybe it's a big rock," said Angus, a pots-and-pans-talent sparrow man. "Though I've certainly never seen a rock this round before."

"Maybe it's a giant black pearl," said Rani. "Though I've never seen a pearl this big."

Tink shook her head. "No," she said. "It would be shiny if it were a pearl."

Dulcie flew hesitantly up to it. She gave it a small rap with her knuckles. "Ow!" she said. "It's hard!" She blew on her hand. "And it's hot!" she added.

Tink didn't like to stand around. And she had stood around long enough. Bravely, she marched up to the ball and gave it a good hard smack.

"It's iron," she said. She shook her hand to cool it off from the hot metal. "Good old-fashioned Never iron."

Several fairies frowned. "Iron is really heavy," Dulcie said worriedly.

"It's going to be hard to move," said Rani. She started to cry.

"We should try to find out where it came from," the queen told them. "That might help us figure out how to get rid of it."

Her suggestion was greeted with enthusiasm. "Let's take a good look at it," said Rani. She wiped the tears from her eyes.

The fairies all moved in closer. They circled the ball. Some fairies flew around the top. Others bent down low to look at the part that touched the ground.

"Hold on!" said Tink. She hovered like a hummingbird near the very top of the ball. "I see something."

Other fairies flew over to join her. "You're right," said Lily, a garden-talent fairy. "It's some kind of a mark."

Angus nodded. "It's almost like a – "

"A hook!" Tink shouted in triumph. "It's a mark that looks like a hook! And you know what that means."

"*Captain Hook!*" cried several fairies.

"Of course. Why didn't I realise it before? It's a cannonball!" Tink declared.

Tink had seen plenty of cannonballs back in the days when she had spent all her time with Peter Pan. But she had never before seen a cannonball in Pixie Hollow. Hook and his pirates never came to this part of Never Land's forest. And the fairies tried to avoid the pirates as much as they could.

Just then, they heard a muffled boom from the direction of Pirate Cove. Several fairies jumped.

"Cannon fire," said Queen Clarion. "Captain Hook must be after Peter Pan again."

The others knew what she meant. On Never Land, there was an on-and-off battle between Hook and his pirates and Peter and the Lost Boys. On certain quiet nights, when the wind was just right, the fairies could hear Pan and Hook's swords clashing in the distance.

"Hmm," said Tink with a worried little frown. Peter Pan was a friend of Tink's. Though she rarely saw him anymore, she knew him better than any of the other fairies did. She didn't like to think of Captain Hook firing cannonballs at Peter.

But Peter is too quick and too clever to get hit by a cannonball, Tink assured herself.

There was another muffled boom, followed by a whizzing sound.

"Everyone, duck!" said the queen.

The fairies all dashed for cover in the roots of the Home Tree. Something flew through the air high over their heads. It landed in the nearby forest with a tremendous thud.

"The fairy circle!" cried Dulcie. She

hurried out from behind a root. "What if it landed there?"

"What about Mother Dove?" Rani said, almost in a whisper. "What if it hit her hawthorn tree?"

The fairies looked at each other in stricken silence. Mother Dove was the closest thing to pure goodness in all of Never Land. She was the source of all the fairies' magic. They had almost lost her once, when a hurricane hit Never Land. The thought of losing her again was too dreadful to bear.

In a tense voice, Queen Clarion told several fast-flying fairies to fly to the hawthorn and check on Mother Dove. They zipped off in a blur.

Moments later, the fast fliers were back.

"Mother Dove is fine," a fast-flying sparrow man reported. "Not one feather ruffled. And the fairy circle is undamaged."

The fairies let out a collective sigh of relief.

Tink glared at the big black cannonball in the courtyard. "How dare those pirates!" she exclaimed. "How could they be so careless? I say – "

But before she could say more, Spring, a message-talent fairy, came speeding up to her. She had a grim look on her face.

"Tink," she said. "I've just been to the top of the Home Tree. I think you'd better come with me."

3

WHAT NOW? Tink wondered. *And what does it have to do with me?*

Maybe something metal has broken, and they need me to fix it, Tink mused. *But why right at this moment?*

She followed the messenger into the Home Tree. They passed through the main corridor, where paintings representing each different Never fairy talent hung on the walls. Tink saw that most of the paintings were crooked. Some had even fallen to the floor. She stopped and straightened the painting of a dented stewpot, which was the symbol for the pots-and-pans talent.

Up through the branches they went. They turned right, then left, then left again. Finally, they came to the corridor that led to Tink's room. Tink saw her friend Terence waiting for her. Terence had been in the group the queen had sent to check the damage to the tree. He looked upset.

"Tink," he said, "I hardly know how to tell you this. Your bedroom – "

Her beloved bedroom! Tink didn't even wait for him to finish his sentence. She zoomed down the corridor to the end of the branch where her room sat. What would she find? she wondered. Would it be a horrible mess? Would her loaf-pan bed be overturned, or even dented? It was not a pleasant thought.

When she reached the tip of the branch, she stopped cold.

Her room wasn't a mess. Her room

wasn't there at all.

Tinker Bell hovered, staring. The walls, the ceiling, and everything in the room had disappeared. All that remained was the floor and the jagged edges of the broken walls.

She looked up past the hole where her ceiling should have been. The surrounding branches had a few broken twigs. But the other fairies' rooms were still there. The cannonball had hit Tink's room, and Tink's alone.

Tink felt faint. She sat down cross-legged on the floor.

How could my room just be... gone? she thought. *Where will I sleep? Where will I keep my clothes and other things? Where* are *my clothes and other things?*

More fairies began to arrive to see

what had happened.

"Oh, Tink," said her friend Beck. "It's awful!"

"I can't believe it," said Prilla. "Your bed is gone. And it was such a great bed."

Tink stood up. She didn't want the other fairies to feel sorry for her. She took a deep breath. "We'll just rebuild it," she said. She sounded calmer than she felt. "And it will be an even better room than before."

"We'll all help you," said Terence. The others nodded in agreement.

Suddenly Tink felt angry. After all, no one would have to rebuild anything if it weren't for the cannonball. Her hands balled into tiny fists thinking about it.

"And in the meantime," she said

fiercely, "we're going to get that horrid cannonball out of our courtyard. What do you say, fairies?"

"Yes!" they all cried. "Let's do it!" With Tink in the lead, the fairies went back to the courtyard. The most obvious thing was to try pushing the cannonball, Tink decided. "If a lot of us get behind it and fly as hard as we can, maybe we can roll it out of the courtyard," she said.

"Let's move every little twig out of its path. That way it won't get stuck on anything," said Beck.

The cleaning-talent fairies grabbed their brooms and swept up all the splinters. Other fairies helped by moving the pieces of the squashed mushroom chairs.

"All right," said Tink. "Let's get into pushing formation."

Several fairies arranged themselves behind the ball. The strongest ones hovered close to the bottom. The weaker ones stayed near the top.

"One, two, three... *shove!*" shouted Tink.

The fairies beat their wings madly. They heaved against the ball as hard as they could.

After a moment, they stopped. Several fairies leaned against the ball, panting.

"I think it moved a tiny, tiny bit," said Prilla, who was inclined to see the best in all situations.

"It didn't move an inch," said Angus, who was not.

"Let's give it another try," said Tink.

They rearranged themselves. Now the strongest fairies went to the top of the ball. The weaker ones went to the bottom.

"One, two, three... *shove!*" Tink cried again.

The fairies used every ounce of strength they had. At last they stopped. Their wings were quivering with exhaustion.

"Nothing," said Angus.

Indeed, the ball had not moved, not a hair.

Tink sighed. "Well, I guess that's not going to work," she said. "But this is only the beginning."

4

AS THE OTHER FAIRIES sat down to rest, Tink began to pace. She was sure she could come up with an idea that would work. She tugged at her bangs, thinking hard.

Down in the meadow near the dairy barn, the faint sound of bells could be heard. Cannonball or no cannonball, the dairy mice had to be fed. The mouse-herding-talent fairies were taking the herd out to pasture.

Tink looked toward the meadow. "Mice!" she said suddenly.

"Mice?" said two of the fairies nearest to her.

"Yes," said Tink. "Mice. It's simple. We'll harness all the dairy mice to the cannonball. Maybe, together, all of them can move it!"

"Wonderful idea, Tink!" said Queen Clarion.

The messenger-talent fairies headed for the pasture to tell the mouse-herding fairies to round up the dairy mice. Meanwhile, the kitchen-talent fairies hurried back to the kitchen to collect all the loaves of acorn bread they could spare. The mice adored acorn bread. Occasionally, a mouse would get loose from the herd and be caught in the Home Tree pantry, nibbling bread. Now the fairies could use the bread as a lure to get the mice to pull the ball.

Fairies from other talents pitched in too. Florian and the rest of the weaving-talent fairies quickly fashioned ropes from sweet grass they'd plucked from the meadow.

"I wish we had time to collect marsh grass," Florian said. "It makes a stronger rope. But I think this should do."

It only took a few minutes for the mouse-herders to get the mice to the Home Tree. One by one, the fairies began to harness the mice to the rope. Altogether, there were thirty-six mice. They stood at attention, their noses quivering.

At last, they were all in formation. The mouse-herding fairies stood just in front of them, waving the bread. The mice squeaked excitedly at the sight and smell of it.

"That's it, my little loves," said one of the mouse herders. "Delicious bread!

Come and get it."

She stepped back a little. The mice strained toward her. "Come on," the fairy urged. "Acorn bread! More than you've ever had before. You can have it all if you just try!"

And the mice did try. They loved that bread more than anything, much more than the sweetgrass seeds they were usually fed. They strained toward the bread. Their little claws dug into the ground. The courtyard echoed with the sounds of their squeaking.

The other fairies cheered them on. "You can do it, mice!" they yelled. "Get the bread! Move the ball! You can do it!"

The ball wobbled. The mice leaned into their harnesses – and the ball moved. Not a lot, maybe half an inch. But it moved.

"It's working, Tink!" cried Terence. He gave her an enormous smile and clapped her on the back.

"It's working! It's working!" other fairies echoed.

Tink's face was flushed. Her eyes shone. All her attention was focused on the cannonball. It moved another half inch, and –

Snap!

The rope around the cannonball broke. The mice leaped forward, suddenly free from the weight. They lunged at the bread in the mouse-herders' hands and quickly began to gobble it down.

The fairies stopped in mid-cheer. Everyone let out a disappointed sigh.

"Marsh grass," said Florian. She shook her head. "It always makes a stronger rope."

Tink flew over to look at the mice. They were still panting from the effort of pulling the ball. Their furry sides heaved in and out.

"Do you think they could do it again?" she asked one of the mouse-herding fairies. "If we made a stronger rope, that is."

The fairy shook her head. "I don't think so," she said. "It might wear them out. Dairy mice can be quite delicate, you know. If they get too tired, they stop giving milk."

Tink's shoulders slumped. But she tried hard not to show her disappointment. "Well," she said, "it was a good try. We'll just have to think of something else."

Queen Clarion spoke up. "Maybe that's enough work for one day," she said gently. "The cannonball won't go anywhere before tomorrow. Why don't we all get cleaned up and have some dinner?"

The fairies murmured their agreement. Not only were they all tired, they were also very hungry.

As the other fairies headed into the Home Tree, Tink lingered behind.

Well, Tink, you wanted a challenge, she said to herself. *And now you've got one.*

She stared up at the huge cannonball. *But am I up to it?* she wondered.

5

BECAUSE THE KITCHEN was such a mess, dinner that night was simple – acorn-butter sandwiches with dandelion salad. The tired fairies ate quickly. The sun had already set. After a long, hard day of work, they were eager to go to bed.

As soon as she was done eating, Tink realised she had a problem. She had nowhere to sleep. She watched as the other fairies headed for their rooms. In all the excitement over the cannonball, they had forgotten that Tink didn't have her own room to go to.

The tearoom slowly emptied. Tink remained sitting at her table. She wasn't sure what to do. As the shadows lengthened, she felt more and more forlorn.

At last Rani noticed Tink sitting alone. She realized the problem at once.

"Tink," she said, "what will you do tonight?"

"I think maybe I'll just sleep outside," Tink replied bravely. "I can use a maple leaf as a blanket."

"You can sleep in my room," Rani told her. "It's better than sleeping outside, anyway."

"Okay," Tink said. She felt relieved. "I would like that. I'm awfully tired."

Tink followed Rani up to her room. She had visited Rani's room many times before. But until that evening, she hadn't noticed the details. She looked around at the blue-green walls and the seaweed curtains hanging in the windows. The floor was paved with smooth river stones.

It seemed like a quiet, peaceful place. Tink was looking forward to a good night's sleep.

"Shall we play a game of seashell tiddlywinks?" Rani asked.

"Not tonight," said Tink. She really was exhausted. "I think I'm ready to go to bed. Where should I sleep?"

"I could pile lots of blankets on the floor," Rani suggested.

"Let me help you," said Tink.

Together they piled woven-fern blankets on the floor until they had made a soft bed.

"That should be very comfortable," Tink said when they were done. But she could not help noticing how humid Rani's room was. Even the blankets felt damp.

Tink settled herself on the pile. She was so tired, she was sure she'd fall asleep in a moment.

Rani covered her up with a sheet, which was also slightly damp. "Good night, dear friend," she said. Then she climbed into her own bed, which was made from driftwood. She pulled the seaweed quilt up to her chin.

Tink lay on her back, gazing at the blue-green ceiling. *It was nice of Rani to take me in*, she thought. Then she closed her eyes and gave in to her tiredness.

Seconds later, Tink opened her eyes. She could feel a lump beneath the pile of blankets. It was one of the river stones that paved the floor.

Tink tried turning on her side, but that was no better. She flopped over on her stomach, but that was worse still. She ended up on her back again.

Tink thought wistfully of her comfy loaf-pan bed and the soft, dappled light that came through the colander lampshades in her room. How she loved to fall asleep beneath the still life of the stockpot, whisk, and griddle. And now it was gone, all gone. Tink sighed.

Moonlight filtered in through the seaweed curtains. Suddenly Tink gasped and jumped up. Two long arms seemed to reach out to her from the corner of the room.

Rani heard her and sat straight up. "What's the matter?" she cried.

"Th-there's something in the corner!" whispered Tink. She was almost too scared to breathe.

"Where? I don't see it!" whispered Rani. She followed the direction of Tink's pointing finger. But the room was too dark. They couldn't see clearly.

Quickly, Rani lit her scallop-shell lamp. Then she started to giggle. "That's just my clothes hanging on a clothes tree, Tink. It's made from a coral branch. Remember?"

Gradually, Tink's heart stopped racing. Her breath returned to normal. "Oh," she said. "So it is." Now she felt foolish. She wished more than ever that she could be in her own bed.

Rani turned out the light. They settled back down to sleep.

Tink tried to drift off, she really did. But the paving rocks were not getting any softer. And then she became aware of another thing.

Drip. Drip. Drip-drip. Drip.

Drip. Drip. Drip-drip. Drip.

It was a slow, steady rhythm. Tink had forgotten all about Rani's drip. She had a permanent leak in her room, whether it was raining or not. Beneath the leak sat a bucket made from a human-sized thimble. Inside the bucket, a Never minnow swam contentedly around and around.

Drip. Drip. Drip-drip. Drip.

By now, Tink had given up trying to sleep. She lay on her back and stared at the ceiling. Every now and then she shifted her wings under the damp sheet to find a better position.

Sometime before dawn, Tink heard a new noise. It was Rani crying.

"Rani," whispered Tink, "are you all right?"

There was no answer, just more crying. Tink brightened her glow so she could see Rani a little better. Rani was sound asleep, weeping onto her pillow. The air in the room was getting damper and damper.

"Rani," Tink tried again. "Wake up. You're having a bad dream."

Still Rani did not wake. Tink finally gave up and went back to staring at the ceiling. She listened to the dripping water and Rani's crying.

A little after dawn, Rani awoke. She sat up in bed and stretched her arms toward the ceiling. "I just had the most wonderful dream!" she said when she saw that Tink was awake.

"No, you didn't. You had an awful dream," Tink snapped. She was fairly cross, having not slept a wink the whole night.

Rani gave her a strange look and shook her head. "No, it was long and wonderful," she said. "I was playing with a big ball of water. I was tossing it back and forth with Silvermist and Tally. We could throw it as high as the top of the Home Tree and make a rainbow in the sunlight. It was so beautiful!"

Now it was Tink's turn to give Rani a strange look. "But you were crying," she insisted. "Cupfuls. Buckets. Barrels. Feel your bed, it's all – "

Rani broke into a big grin. " – wet," she finished. "I was crying in the dream, too! Crying from happiness!"

Tink just shook her head. She got up from her damp, lumpy bed. "Rani," she said, "you are my very good friend. But I am a pots-and-pans fairy and you are a water fairy, and I will never truly understand you." She smiled and gave Rani a hug.

Rani's eyes filled with tears again. "You're my good friend, too. And I'll never really understand you, either," she said, hugging Tink back. She wiped her eyes with a leafkerchief. "Do you want to go have some breakfast?"

"Yes," said Tink. "But my wings are too damp to fly."

Rani picked up another leafkerchief

and gently dried Tink's wings. Then they went downstairs for breakfast.

6

BREAKFAST WAS VERY GOOD, as usual. Platters of Dulcie's wonderful pumpkin muffins and pots of blackberry tea sat on every table in the tearoom. But no breakfast would have been delicious enough to cheer Tink up that morning.

Tink was tired. She was damp. And she wanted her room back.

She stared gloomily at the serving platter in front of her. It reminded her of her platter–frying-pan–spoon chair.

"Rough night?" asked Angus. He was sitting next to Tink at the pots-and-pans-talent table.

"Just a little damp," said Tink with a sigh. She took a sip of tea. "But don't worry. I'm ready to get to work. I'll have that cannonball out of Pixie Hollow in no time." Even to her own ears, she did not sound very sure.

"Tinker Bell!" a cheerful voice exclaimed. Tink turned around. Gwinn, a tiny decoration-talent fairy, was beaming at her. "Are you ready to start putting your room back together?" Gwinn asked. "Cedar and I are heading up there now to get started." She gestured at Cedar, who was standing behind her.

Cedar was the biggest, strongest-looking fairy Tinker Bell had ever seen. She was nearly six inches tall! It was clear from the hammer and saw Cedar was carrying that she was a carpenter-talent fairy.

Cedar nodded shyly in greeting.

Her great height made Gwinn look even tinier.

"Usually, we prepare rooms for fairies who have just arrived in Never Land," Gwinn continued. She spoke very, very fast. Tink had to concentrate to keep up. "Of course, we don't know them yet. So we just make our best guess about what that fairy might want. And then we hope she likes it. But you're already *here!* I've never helped a fairy decorate her own room before! You can tell me exactly what you want! It will be perfect! *Perfect!* Right, Cedar?"

Cedar nodded and stared bashfully at the ground.

Tink bit her lip. She wanted to start rebuilding her room. But she had promised to get rid of the cannonball.

Angus read her mind. "You can work on the cannonball later, Tink, after you and Gwinn decide what your new room should look like," he pointed out.

Tink thought about it for a moment. Angus was right. The cannonball could wait.

"All right," Tink said. She smiled. "Let's go!"

A short time later, Tink was watching Cedar hammer planks into the walls of her new room.

Gwinn flew from one corner to the next, measuring the space with her eyes. She kept up a steady stream of chatter.

"You'll want silver paint," Gwinn told Tink. "Or maybe gold. Or something copper? Ooh, yes! Copper could be just lovely with the sunlight coming in – "

"Silver will be fine," said Tink, trying to keep up.

"And I suppose you'd like colander lampshades again," Gwinn went on. "Although a nice iris-petal lantern would give the room a softer look... "

"Colanders, please," Tink cut in. She was surprised to find she was having fun.

"And you'll need curtains, a bedspread, some kind of rug... " Gwinn zipped from corner to corner. She was making Tink dizzy.

Tink sat down in the middle of the bare floor to watch her.

Gwinn will make sure that the walls are the right color, Tink thought. *And she will get new colanders for the lamps.* But Gwinn couldn't make her another stilllife painting. And Cedar couldn't make her another loaf-pan bed.

If I want my room back just the way it was, Tink thought, *I'm going to have to take matters into my own hands.*

"I'll be back in a little while," she told Gwinn and Cedar.

Cedar mumbled good-bye through a mouthful of nails. Gwinn absent-mindedly waved some curtain fabric at her. Tink flew out through the open ceiling and over the woods of Pixie Hollow.

Soon, Tink arrived at Bess's studio. It was made from an old tangerine crate that the art-talent fairy had set up in a remote clearing in the woods, where she could paint in peace and quiet.

Tink found Bess hard at work. She

was painting a portrait of an animal-talent fairy. The animal-talent fairy posed on a cushion, holding her favorite ladybird on her lap.

"Tink!" Bess said. She set down her brush and hugged her friend. "What a terrible thing to happen to your room. Is there anything I can do to help?"

"Actually, there is," said Tink. She explained that she needed another still life of a stockpot, whisk, and griddle to hang over her bed.

Bess looked a little embarrassed. "Oh, Tink," she said unhappily. "Of *course* I'll paint a new picture for you. But I won't be able to get to it for a while. I've already promised paintings to five other fairies."

The animal-talent fairy cleared her

throat impatiently. The ladybug on her lap was getting restless. Bess gave Tink another hug, and then got back to work.

Tink flew off, trying not to feel discouraged. Her next stop was the kitchen. She hoped to find some pots and pans that were beyond repair. With luck, she could make another frying-pan chair exactly like her old one.

Dulcie met Tink at the kitchen door. She was carrying a tray of pretty little tea cakes. As Dulcie set the cakes on a windowsill to cool, Tink asked her if she had any pots, pans, spoons, whisks, or other kitchen items that she needed to get rid of.

"Well," replied Dulcie, "there was that salad fork with the bent tines. I was ready to give up on it. But Angus fixed it last week. It's been perfectly pointy and prongy ever since."

The other pots-and-pans fairies are too good at their jobs, Tink thought. She tugged at her bangs and gave a frustrated sigh. She didn't want to make a chair out of objects that were still useful.

Tink could usually fix almost anything. But here was something that couldn't be fixed, at least not right away.

"Grrr!" cried Tink. She shot three inches into the air with sheer frustration. Her room was smashed, and even when it was fixed, it still wouldn't feel like her room. After all, *where* was she going to find another loaf-pan bed?

That cannonball will regret the day it fell into Pixie Hollow, Tink vowed. *And Captain Hook will regret it even more.*

7

TINK ZOOMED into the courtyard. She flew right up to the cannonball and gave it a mighty kick.

Ow! Tink danced through the air, clutching her toes and grimacing in pain. A few fairies who had been flying by stared at Tink in astonishment.

Once her toes stopped hurting, Tink found that she felt much calmer. But now she was more determined than ever to get rid of the big, bad ball.

"This cannonball is going to move!" she cried. "I am going to banish it from Pixie Hollow once and for all. But I'm going to need help from every fairy and sparrow man. Together, we can do it! Now, who's with me?"

But the other fairies didn't jump up as Tink hoped they would.

"I don't know. Maybe we could learn to live with the cannonball," said one of the decoration-talent fairies. "We could probably fix it up to make it look nice."

The other decoration-talent fairies brightened a bit. "We could!" one agreed. "We could decorate it with hollyhock garlands and daisy chains."

"Or we could paint it a pretty shade of green to sort of blend in," said another. "Maybe a nice sage color."

"But… but don't you want to get rid of it?" Tink asked, astonished.

"Well, of course we do, Tink," said Beck, who happened to be in the courtyard. "But we want to get back to doing what we usually do. We're all busy with our own talents."

Tink couldn't believe what she was hearing. Were the other fairies giving up already, before they'd even tried?

"We have fun in the courtyard, don't we?" she said. "It's part of our home. How will we feel looking at this cannonball every time we come out of the Home Tree? We'll never be able to have a meeting or a party here again. Even if it's decorated and painted, it will still take up too much room."

Several fairies murmured in agreement. But no one volunteered to help.

"We tried moving it yesterday, and we couldn't," a water-talent sparrow man pointed out.

"I know we can do this," Tink

replied. "We just have to figure out how."

Just then, Terence flew up. He was holding a teacup in one hand. In his other hand was a sack of fairy dust.

"Tink, you didn't get your fairy dust yet today, did you?" he said.

As a dust-talent sparrow man, Terence handed out dust to all the fairies and sparrow men in Pixie Hollow. Everyone got one teacupful per day. The dust was what allowed the fairies to fly and do magic.

As Terence poured the magical dust over Tink, her eyes widened. "That's it! I know how we can move the cannonball!" she cried.

The fairies in the courtyard perked up. "How, Tink?" Terence asked.

"We move big things with balloon

carriers, right?" Tink said. Balloon carriers were baskets attached to fairy-dust-filled balloons. The fairies used them to move things that were too heavy to carry. "That's what we'll do with the cannonball. We'll build a giant balloon and use lots of extra fairy dust to give it more lift. We can float the cannonball away."

"It's a good idea," said Terence. The other fairies nodded. Even Angus looked impressed.

"Send word to the other dust-talent fairies," Tink told Terence. "We'll need all the fairy dust they can spare. The rest of us will get the balloon carrier ready."

This was easier said than done. In order to attach the balloon to the cannonball, they would need heavy ropes. Tink found Florian and explained her plan.

"We'll use marsh grass this time," Florian said with certainty. "And we'll make it extra thick."

She got the weaving-talent fairies together, and they set out to collect long strands of tough marsh grasses, which they would weave into the strongest ropes they could make.

Next, Tink went to the sewing-talent fairies. She asked them to make a silk balloon, the biggest one Pixie Hollow had ever seen.

Some of the fairies grumbled. They didn't want to leave the pretty petal dresses and leaf-frock coats they were working on. But Tink's spirit was catching. Soon, they were collecting every spare scrap of spider silk to make the giant balloon.

It was afternoon by the time the weaving-talent fairies finished making the ropes. But they looked sturdy this time. They were nearly as thick as a fairy's waist.

The weavers secured the ropes around the bottom of the cannonball. Then it was time to attach the balloon. The sewing-talent fairies sewed the ends of each rope to the edges of the balloon.

Tink oversaw all this work. She paced back and forth, worrying. Would the balloon lift off? Would the cannonball stay attached? What if this idea didn't work either?

At last, the whole contraption was ready to go. It was time for the dust-talent fairies and sparrow men to do their work.

By now a crowd had gathered. Everyone watched, hardly daring to breathe, as Terence and a dust-talent sparrow man named Jerome began to fill the balloon with fairy dust. Instead of the teacups they usually used to hand out the dust, they scooped up great mounds of it with shovels they had borrowed from the garden-talent fairies.

The balloon started to rise – up, up, up. The fairies watched in wonder. Soon the balloon was completely inflated. It strained against the ropes.

The ropes pulled taut, but the cannonball stayed stubbornly on the ground.

"More fairy dust!" cried Tink.

Terence and Jerome flew up to the top of the balloon and sprinkled more shovelfuls of dust onto it. They sprinkled some dust onto the cannonball for good measure. The balloon strained harder and harder. All the fairies and sparrow men strained with it. Their muscles were tense. Their wings vibrated in sheer concentration. The fairies glowed brightly as they willed the balloon to rise.

And finally, it did! The grass ropes pulled tauter, and the cannonball could resist no longer. It lifted off the ground.

"It's going!" shouted Tink.

First it rose just a hair off the ground, no more than the thickness of a fairy's wing. Then it reached the height of two hairs. Then it was almost as high up as a fairy's knee, and then higher than a fairy's head. It was working! It was really working!

If the fairies and sparrow men had not been so caught up in the progress of the cannonball, they might have noticed that a strong breeze had sprung up. But they did not notice, until –

Pow!

Hisssssss.

"What was that?" Tink cried in alarm.

What it was, they soon discovered, was a horse chestnut. The spiky green globe had fallen from a nearby horse chestnut tree. And the wind had been blowing in just the right direction to push it into the balloon. The horse chestnut's spikes had pierced the delicate spider silk.

The hissing lasted only a second. The cannonball landed back in the courtyard with a great thud. Inside the tree, delicate cups and saucers could be heard shattering in the tearoom.

The fairies groaned.

"Well, that's the end of that," Angus said.

But that wasn't the end. For the cannonball had gotten just the start it needed. It began to roll.

8

"THE BALL!" Rani cried. "L-look out!"

Several fairies leaped out of the way in the nick of time. There was a very slight slope away from the Home Tree, but that was enough. The cannonball rolled down it.

"Hooray!" a decoration-talent fairy yelled. "Good-bye, ball!"

"Good riddance!" added a butterfly herder. Other fairies joined in the cheering.

But Tink followed the ball's progress, frowning.

"It's great that we got it going, but – " she began.

"Now we don't know *where* it's going," Rani finished for her.

"Exactly," said Tink.

The ball began to pick up speed. The fairies' cheers died out.

"It was so hard to start," Terence said worriedly. "But now it's going to be impossible to stop!"

"Maybe it will just roll into a tree or something," said Beck.

"If we're lucky," said Angus.

"I think we'd better follow it!" cried Tink. And the fairies leaped into the air to chase after the ball.

The cannonball was rolling fast now. It bounced across a tree root and rolled over a hillock of grass. It was headed for Havendish Stream.

"It's going to hit the mill!" cried Jerome.

This was truly a disaster. The mill

was one of the most important places in Pixie Hollow. The tree-picking-talent fairies ground grains and nuts into baking flour there. And the dust-talent fairies used the mill to grind Mother Dove's feathers into fairy dust. It was also where the fairy dust was stored – all of it. An entire year's supply.

At once, the same picture flashed through every fairy and sparrow man's mind: the mill smashed, the fairy dust inside blowing away with the wind. They would be unable to fly, unable to do magic. How would they even build another mill if they did not have the power of fairy dust?

A startled rabbit poked his head out of his burrow. But when he saw the cannonball rolling toward him, he quickly dove back inside.

The cannonball rolled over a large toadstool, flattening it. The fairies flew helplessly behind. They could hardly bring themselves to watch.

But just before it reached the mill, the cannonball hit a good-sized rock. It jumped into the air and changed course. Instead of crashing into the mill, the ball splashed into the stream just above it. And there it stopped, wedged against the bank.

The fairies breathed sighs of relief all around. They laughed and hugged each other with joy. The mill was saved!

But Tink was not laughing. She did not take her eyes from the ball. As she watched, the water of Havendish Stream began to back up around it.

"Oh, no!" she said. "The stream is blocked!"

Everyone stared in disbelief. Tink was right. The ball had landed in the narrow branch of the stream that fed the mill. The water slowed to a trickle.

A few minnows had been thrown from the stream by the force of the cannonball's splash. They lay flopping on the bank. With cries of alarm, the animal-talent fairies raced to help them. They scooped the little fish up in their hands and dropped them back in the water.

This was not good. Not good at all. If the stream stopped running, the mill wheel would stop turning.

Indeed, they all heard the mill grind to a stop.

Rani started to cry, and it was not from happiness.

Why didn't I think of this? Tink asked herself angrily. *Why didn't it occur to me that once the ball started rolling, it was anybody's guess where it would end up?*

She sank down to the ground. She felt completely defeated. She had taken on a challenge that was too big. And she had failed. What was going to happen to Pixie Hollow now?

"Well, Tink," someone said. Tink looked up. Queen Clarion was standing next to her. "I guess it's time for you to come up with another idea," the queen said seriously.

This took Tink by surprise. She had thought the story was over. The ball was stuck in the stream. There was certainly no way to move it now.

But Rani was nodding and smiling through her tears. "We know you can figure this out, Tink," she said. "Look how many things you've already thought of. There has to be one more thing."

Tink was astounded. Not only did the others have hope that the problem could be solved, they thought she could solve it.

Rani is right, she thought. *There has to be one more thing.* Tink knew she had a responsibility to figure out what that one thing was. The other fairies were counting on her.

"Yes, Tink," said Florian. "It's time for your next idea. Do you want us to leave you alone?"

"Or would you like some nice

soup while you think?" said one of the cooking-talent fairies, who specialised in cucumber soup.

"No soup," Tink said, squaring her shoulders. "I'm just going to think."

9

TINK FLITTED around the whole terrible scene, trying to focus. It was hard looking at the mess the cannonball had made. Water was starting to flood the banks of the stream, turning them into muddy pools. Toadstools and wildflowers had been squashed and flattened when the ball rolled over them. The cannonball had also plowed through a pile of acorns that the tree-picking-talent fairies had set aside to be ground in the mill. Now little chips of acorn littered the landscape.

Tink stared at them. They reminded her of something.

Little chips of acorn, she thought. *Little chips...*

"I've got it!" she hollered. "I've got

the solution! I was thinking about it the wrong way the whole time! The cannonball is a huge thing, right?" said Tink. "It was much too heavy for us to move. And we certainly couldn't control it once it started moving. But even if we can't move a huge thing, we can move lots of *little* things."

Queen Ree nodded her head in understanding. "Of course!" she said.

"Of course *what?*" said a few fairies who hadn't caught on.

"We're going to break the cannonball into lots of tiny pieces and move them out of Pixie Hollow," Tink declared.

"Spring!" She turned to the message-talent fairy. "Ask the other pots-and-pans fairies to bring all the hammers and chisels they have in their workshops. And the carpenter-talent fairies – they have hammers and chisels, too!"

"I have a couple of chisels," said an art-talent fairy. "For making sculptures."

"Great!" said Tink. "Let's round up all the tools we have. We're going to break this cannonball up!"

A short time later, an array of tools was laid out on the grass next to the cannon-ball. The sand-sorting-talent fairies had piled sandbags around the ball, to hold back the stream. That way, the fairies wouldn't get wet as they worked.

Tink grabbed a hammer and chisel and flew to the top of the cannonball. As the best pots-and-pans fairy in Pixie Hollow, Tink knew a lot about metal. For example, she knew that every piece of metal had a weak point.

She put her ear close to the cannonball. Then she began to tap it with her hammer, inching across the surface.

Bing, bing, bing, bing, bing, bing, bing, bing, bing, bing, bong, bing…

Tink stopped. She went back and tapped the spot again.

Bong!

Tink had found the cannonball's weak spot. Holding the tip of her chisel against the ball, Tink whacked it with the hammer as hard as she could. A crack appeared.

Tink whacked it again. The crack grew.

"Everybody take a hammer and chisel!" Tink told the other fairies. "Even if your talent is completely unrelated to breaking up cannonballs, give it a try. You might like it."

The fairies got to work. As they wedged their chisels into the iron, more cracks appeared. The air started to ring with the sound of metal banging into metal. It was a sound Tink loved with all her heart.

"I like this!" said one of the cooking-talent fairies, whose specialty was making ice sculptures. "It's just like chipping ice. But you don't have to be careful!"

Gradually, the cracks in the cannonball grew. Pieces began to break off. The fairies laid them on the bank of Havendish Stream.

Soon they had broken the whole cannonball apart. A mound of iron bits sat by the stream.

"What are we going to do with all this?" said Twire, a scrap-metal-recovery-talent fairy. "It's more iron than we could use in an entire year in Pixie Hollow."

Tink nodded. But she wasn't really focused on what Twire was saying. She was getting another idea.

Quietly, she waved Terence over. "I want to ask your opinion about something," she said. "About fairy-dust magic." She whispered her idea into Terence's ear.

Terence scratched his head thoughtfully.

"I think it can be done," he said finally. "It will take a great deal of fairy dust. And the magic won't be easy. We'll have to concentrate. But I think it could work."

"That's what I hoped," said Tink.

She flew back to where the other fairies were still working. They were almost finished breaking apart the cannonball.

Tink stood on one of the bigger pieces of iron to make her announcement.

"Fairies," she said, "we're going to get this cannonball out of Pixie Hollow once and for all."

The fairies cheered.

"But what are we going to do with it?" asked Rani.

Tink smiled and said with a wink, "We're going to give it back to Captain Hook, of course."

10

SHOUTING WITH GLEE, the fairies gathered up the pieces of cannonball. There were many more pieces than there were fairies. So each fairy took as many as she could fly with. Gwinn took one big piece. Cedar took six small ones. Tink herself carried three pieces, and it took all her strength to lift off.

Meanwhile, Jerome and Terence were inside the mill filling sacks full of fairy dust, as much as they could carry.

When everything was ready, the fairies lifted into the air. It was quite a sight, for those who could see it: a great cloud of fairies flying over the lush landscape of Never Land, headed for Pirate Cove. Of course, the pirates themselves could not see the fairies, who were invisible to them. If Captain Hook had looked up just then, he would have seen hundreds of chips of iron miraculously bobbing through the air.

But Captain Hook was not looking up. As the fairies approached the cove, they could see the vile-tempered pirate rowing a small boat through the water near the shore. He was muttering to himself.

"I'll teach that ridiculous boy a lesson," he growled. "Throw my best cutlass into the sea, will he? Thinks he can get the best of me, does he? Well, we'll see about that, Master Peter Pan. Let's see how you like a cannonball for your dinner tonight."

As Hook rowed, he looked down through the shallow water. Evidently, he was trying to find his lost cutlass.

The fairies were right above Hook's little rowboat. They hovered there, still in a cloud. "Okay!" Tink cried. "Start bringing the pieces together!"

The fairies flew nearer to each other. They began to fit the pieces of cannonball together.

"Now the fairy dust!" Tink commanded.

Terence and the other dust-talent fairies and sparrow men began to throw handfuls of fairy dust over the ball. Magically, the iron chips snapped into place like pieces of a jigsaw puzzle. The fairies concentrated, using all the magic they could muster.

In moments, the cannonball was complete. It was just as it had been when it crashed into Pixie Hollow.

And, of course, once it was whole, it was too heavy for the fairies to hold any longer. It fell from their grasp and plummeted toward Captain Hook's rowboat.

Hook looked up just in time to see a cannonball fall from thin air.

"What – " was all he had time to say before the ball crashed into the floor of his rowboat. It broke through the wood and fell to the bottom of the sea.

At once, the boat filled with water. Hook had no choice but to abandon ship. He swam to shore as the rowboat slowly sank.

The sun was setting as the fairies flew back to Pixie Hollow, glad to finally be rid of the cannonball.

The next day, Pixie Hollow had just about returned to normal. Havendish Stream flowed between its banks, which looked none the worse for wear. The mill was turning once again. And fairies from several different talents had pitched in to help repair the courtyard.

The cooking-talent fairies had spent the day making acorn soup, muffins, cookies, and bread with the acorns that had been smashed by the cannonball. Everyone was good and sick of acorns. But all the broken ones had been just about used up, and nothing had gone to waste.

After her wet night in Rani's room, Tink had decided to sleep outside until her room was rebuilt. She'd found a nook between two branches where she would be sheltered from the wind and safe from owls. She had actually been quite happy out there, looking at the stars through the leaves of the Home Tree.

And in the morning, what had she found by the roots of a nearby tree but her loaf-pan bed! It had one big dent in it. *Challenging to fix,* Tink thought. *But not too challenging.*

Later that day, Gwinn and Cedar helped Tink carry the bed up to her new room. They had worked all night to get it ready for her.

When Gwinn opened the door, Tink was speechless with delight. Her new room had colander lamps just like the old ones. The walls were painted with silver paint to make them look as if they were made of tin. And best of all, Bess had manged to finish a new painting for Tink after all. It was another still life of a stockpot, whisk, and griddle – and it was twice the size of the old one.

"It's beautiful," she managed to say at last.

Gwinn and Cedar helped Tink put her bed back into place. Then Gwinn took another look around the room. "You know," she said thoughtfully, "we could decorate with tiny cannonballs, Tink. So you'd always remember your greatest challenge."

"It's an interesting thought," said Tink. "But I'm all through with cannonballs."

Just then, Dulcie came hurrying up to Tink's room. She poked her head in the open door and waved a metal sheet.

"Tink," she said, "do you think you could fix this baking sheet for me? I have one last batch of acorn cookies to put in the oven. It just has a little hole. I know it's hardly worth your attention. Not much of a challenge."

"Believe me," said Tink, "that is just fine with me."

And taking the sheet from Dulcie's hands, she headed for her workshop, whistling.

Join Tinker Bell, Prilla and all
the other Never Fairies in
the next Disney Fairies book...

Fira and the
Full Moon

Here is a fairy-sized preview
of the first chapter!

Fira
and the
Full Moon

1

FIRA STUMBLED UP THE STAIRS to her bedroom in the Home Tree. Her wings dragged on the ground. Her fairy glow had dimmed to a faint glimmer.

Fira was a light-talent fairy. Usually, she glowed especially brightly. But that day she felt too tired to use extra light energy. She felt too tired to fly. Too tired to do anything.

She yawned and stretched her arms

wide. Fira had been working hard lately. All the light-talent fairies had. It was a busy time of year. The bushes and plants in Pixie Hollow were bursting with berries and seeds. Harvest-talent fairies worked late into the night, gathering the plentiful crops. So the light-talent fairies' special glows were needed more than ever.

There were celebrations and festivals, where light talents put on dazzling light shows and performed shadow-puppet plays. And long after the sun had set each day, Fira and her friends helped light the orchards and gardens as the harvest-talent fairies worked.

Just that day, the fairies had finished the harvesting. Overflowing baskets filled the Home Tree kitchen and pantry. The work was done. Now Fira was looking forward to a long nap.

Finally, Fira reached her room. Kicking off her petal shoes, she flopped facedown on her bed.

The late-afternoon sunlight shone through Fira's bedroom window. Even though she was ready to sleep – *more than ready*, Fira thought – she didn't close her pine-needle blinds. A light-talent fairy always liked to have a little sunshine brightening a room.

Fira slipped under her dandelion-fluff blanket. All around Pixie Hollow, she knew, Never fairies were working and playing. Cooking-talent fairies prepared the evening meal in the Home Tree kitchen. Art-talent fairies painted and sculpted in their studios. Wing-washing talents cleaned fairies' wings. Fairies milked the dairy mice in the dairy barn and herded caterpillars in the field.

Not me, Fira thought. *I'm not doing anything.*

She closed her eyes. Before she had another thought, she fell fast asleep.

Knock! Knock!

Fira flew out of bed, bumping her head on the ceiling.

"What?" she cried. "What is it?"

"I'm sorry, Fira." Spring, a message-talent fairy, poked her head through the open window. "I didn't know you were sleeping. You're needed at the Firefly Thicket."

Fira sat down on her bed. "What's going on?" she asked sleepily.

"I'm not sure. But there's some sort of firefly trouble."

Spring gave an apologetic wave and took off.

"Firefly trouble," Fira repeated. That didn't sound good.

Each night, a group of specially trained fireflies flew around Pixie Hollow. They landed on tiny torches, giving light to the fairies and sparrow men.

These fireflies were Fira's responsibility. She took pride in training them, and training them well. She liked being in charge. But just this once, maybe, she could ask Luna or Iridessa to take over. It would be so nice to keep sleeping.

No, no, no. Fira shook her head. *If you want something done right, you should do it yourself,* she thought. Not that she didn't trust her friends. Of course she did. But still…

She sighed. If only she could rest a little while longer. Light-talent fairies' glows were weakest when they were tired. Fira hated when her glow was dim. She liked to light up a room. Maybe her short nap had been enough. She stood and gathered her strength.

Then she flew out into the afternoon. Fira slowed as she got close to Havendish Stream. The Firefly Thicket was in a dense, leafy spot along the far bank. Fira darted around a clump of bushes. Then she spied the entrance, a wide opening in the branches.

"Hello?" she called softly. She ducked her head inside. It was always dark back there. That was why the fireflies liked it.

"Moth!"

Moth was Fira's nickname. Other

fairies joked that she loved light like a moth loved a candle flame.

"Over here, Moth." Beck, a friend of Fira's, waved her over. Beck was an animal-talent fairy. She could communicate with all the animals in Never Land.

"I'm glad you're here, Fira," said Elixa, a healing-talent fairy. "You need to know what's going on."

Fira gazed around. The fireflies rested fitfully on branches. Their lights flickered dimly. Some didn't light at all.

Beck patted the wings of one firefly. Elixa placed a leaf compress on another.

"They have the no-fire flu," Elixa explained. "They won't be able to light Pixie Hollow tonight."

Fira groaned. It was almost dusk.

Already the light-talent fairies would be hanging glowworm lanterns. But the lanterns were only decoration. The fireflies did the real work of lighting Pixie Hollow. This was trouble, indeed.

Beck went to her side. "I know you're tired from all the harvesting," she said quietly, trying not to disturb the fireflies. "But is there anything you can do?"

Fira straightened her wings. "Of course there's something I can do!"

She would organise all the light-talent fairies. They would need to light the places fireflies usually brightened: gardens, groves, busy sky routes. And the next night a full moon would be out, which meant there would be a dance in the fairy circle. The light-talent fairies would have to light that, too. There was so much work! She had to get going!

With a quick wave good-bye, Fira set off once again. Her mind raced with details. Which fairies would light the fairy-dust mill? Which ones would cover the forest? And who would light the fairy circle?

It was a lot to ask of fairies who were already tired. *It will be all right*, Fira told herself. *We can manage for now. But what if the fireflies are still sick tomorrow?*

Collect all the Disney Fairies books

Discover the story of the Never Fairies in
Fairy Dust and the Quest for the Egg

What I Was

meg
rosoff

PENGUIN BOOKS

PENGUIN BOOKS

Published by the Penguin Group
Penguin Books Ltd, 80 Strand, London WC2R 0RL, England
Penguin Group (USA) Inc., 375 Hudson Street, New York, New York 10014, USA
Penguin Group (Canada), 90 Eglinton Avenue East, Suite 700, Toronto, Ontario, Canada M4P 2Y3
(a division of Pearson Penguin Canada Inc.)
Penguin Ireland, 25 St Stephen's Green, Dublin 2, Ireland (a division of Penguin Books Ltd)
Penguin Group (Australia), 250 Camberwell Road, Camberwell, Victoria 3124, Australia
(a division of Pearson Australia Group Pty Ltd)
Penguin Books India Pvt Ltd, 11 Community Centre, Panchsheel Park, New Delhi – 110 017, India
Penguin Group (NZ), 67 Apollo Drive, Rosedale, North Shore 0632, New Zealand
(a division of Pearson New Zealand Ltd)
Penguin Books (South Africa) (Pty) Ltd, 24 Sturdee Avenue, Rosebank, Johannesburg 2196, South Africa

Penguin Books Ltd, Registered Offices: 80 Strand, London WC2R 0RL, England

www.penguin.com

First published 2007
Published in this edition 2008
Reissued 2010
This edition produced for The Book People Ltd,
Hall Wood Avenue, Haydock, St Helens. WA11 9UL

001

Text copyright © Meg Rosoff, 2007
Map copyright © David Atkinson, 2007
Extract from *The Bride's Farewell* copyright © 2009
All rights reserved

The moral right of the author and illustrator has been asserted

Set in Sabon by Palimpsest Book Production Limited, Grangemouth, Stirlingshire
Made and printed in England by Clays Ltd, St Ives plc

British Library Cataloguing in Publication Data
A CIP catalogue record for this book is available from the British Library

ISBN: 978-0-141-34942-8

www.greenpenguin.co.uk